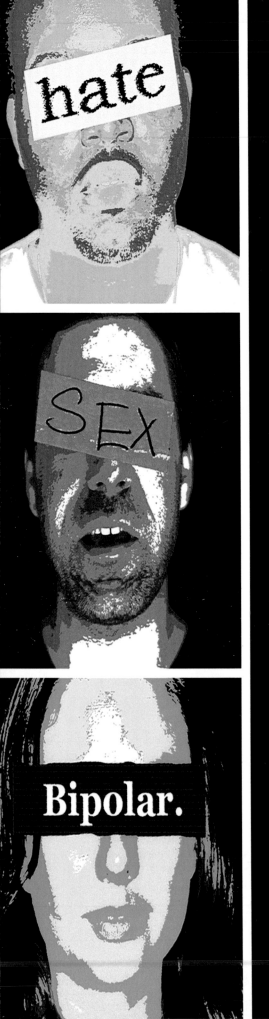

"What if you make a mistake and everyone in your junior high hates you now? How do you deal with that...?"

A young girl -- shyly insecure yet more beautiful than she knows -- nervously stands in the back row of the McHenry Public Library's lecture hall and waits for my answer...but I am at a silent loss. No matter how many times I ask for questions at the end of one of my anti-bullying workshops, I am always thrown when someone kicks off the conversation with a question so bold, personal and raw. Whenever that happens, I don't know what to say.

But the beautiful thing is that I don't have to say anything. Because without fail -- a stranger in the audience will turn around and begin telling that young girl a personal story about how they overcame a mistake they once made...and then someone else will follow up that stranger's story with their own bullied tale...and so on and so on...and before you know it, I am no longer giving a lecture. Everyone has turned their chairs inward, and people are exchanging stories and confessing secrets to complete strangers.

Although rare, that young girl in the McHenry Public Library is not alone in her courage. In each workshop I give, there is always one person whose bravery breathes life into the room: a homeless transgender teenager in a Dallas Baptist church, an addict on his thirteenth trip to rehab in a Reno detox, an elderly man with late-stage AIDS in a WeHo synagogue, an abused wife in a Seattle shelter. While some may see these individuals as broken beings, I embrace them as uniquely courageous inspirations, for they are the ones who motivate us to give voice to our own personal pain.

If we were all more like them, the AnonymoUS Initiative wouldn't exist. There would be no need for a secret letter-writing campaign that allows people to open up about the things that break, shake, scare, scar and bully them -- because we would do that naturally. But sadly, we don't live in a world where words come that easy. Often, our scars fall silent and we keep the things that bully us locked inside.

Perhaps that is human nature, or maybe it is the emotional ramifications of a society that prefers to sweep non-pleasantries under the rug. I don't know; and frankly, knowing that doesn't matter. What does matter is that we -- as individuals, communities and a society at large -- find and foster ways to connect that embrace resiliency and yet don't shy away from life's painful, universal truths.

letter-writing campaign began in March of 2011, we have received over 10,000 letters, emails and art pieces from around the world -- people answering the simple question: "What is it that Bullies You?" This second anthology is a collection of 99 more of these secret confessions. I continue to keep them anonymous because I still believe that what bullies each of us does not define us; these scars are merely one story in the millions of stories that color who we are.

I have attempted to do something unique with this edition, subtly pairing letters with similar stories on opposing pages. While their commonalities might otherwise go unnoticed, it's my aim to show that -- although the facts of our problem-saturated narrative may be different -- the pain behind them often rings the same.

For me, these letters are the proof that bullying isn't just a "gay thing" or "teenage problem." All of us -- all ages, all demographics, all races of the rainbow -- are wrestling with an internal critic, an inner bully, something that leaves us feeling lonely; and ultimately, all we desire is the chance to be heard, to release those scars into the world. Because once we find a way to give voice to our pain, it becomes shared. That toxic shame is no longer our own, and we are empowered by the understanding that we are not alone.

I understand that not all of the things that "bully" us "get better" with time. Some hardships stay with us for life; the journey towards healing is not about overcoming them but learning how to live with them. My hope with these letters is that you allow them to touch your heart, that you find the courage to empathize with the emotion behind each story -- the guilt, the sadness, the anger, the loneliness, the regret, the emotional fallout from mistakes made -- and remember the last time you felt that very same way.

Because when we truly allow ourselves to experience someone else's pain -- when we don't try to fix their problems but simply give witness as they attempt to make sense out of the senseless in their life -- it is only then that we realize how truly connected we are.

And in that connection we find the proof that we are not alone. Even in our darkest moments, we are never alone...and sometimes that's all we need to know.

-Michael Anthony, Creative Director
www.IAmAnonymoUS.org

MY SON ~~THOUGHT~~ THOUGHT
DRUGS WERE MORE
ATTRACTIVE THAN
HIS 4 CHILDREN, SO
NOW I AM RAISING
THEM. IT IS A
BLESSING BUT IT IS
ALSO THE WORST
THING THAT HAS EVER
HAPPENED TO ME AND
MY HUSBAND! I AM 68.
I AM TIRED. BUT
WHAT ELSE ARE YOU
GOING TO DO??????

My HusBand was killed
by a drunk driver
On the way to our
wedding reception

I forgive the driver
but HATE Myself

Strange

I tried to hire a
prostitute once.
She saw my dick
and gave me my
money back.

TRUE STORY!!!!!!!!!

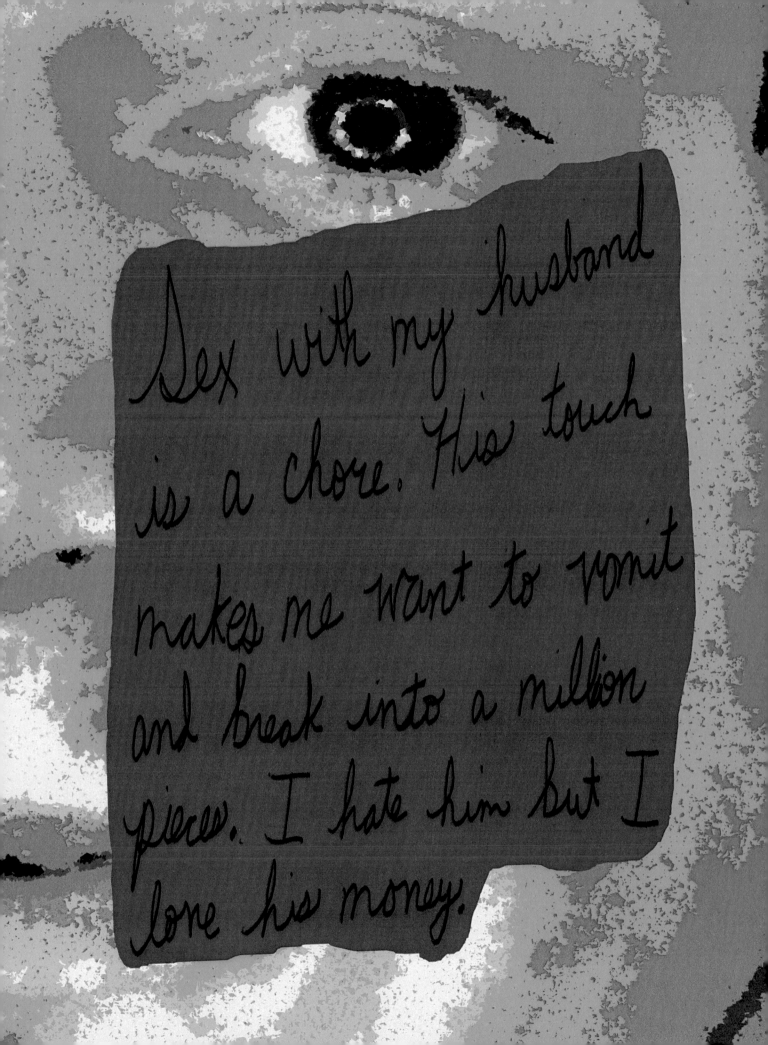

"Bring My Daddy Home".

Love Chelsea

The Good and the Bad of a Deployment
(or, The Musings of a Military Wife)

I can watch whatever I want on TV without heavy sighs and rolled eyes. But then there's no one to laugh about the stupid commercials with.

I have the whole bed to myself. There's no kicking, snoring, or other strange noises that emanate from him. But it's cold in that big bed. And REALLY quiet.

I don't have to shave my legs because I really don't care if they are hairy. But since I'll be celibate for a year no one else cares either.

The grocery bill goes down with one less grown man to feed. But feeding people is how I tell them I love them.

I don't have to watch the news anymore. But I CAN'T watch the news because I'm afraid that's how I'll find out he's died.

Since we have two daughters it's girl time ALL THE TIME! But since we have two daughters it's girl time ALL THE TIME!

The trash will be put out on time. But it will be put out on time by me.

People will be sympathetic. But I don't want their sympathy. All I really want is the number for a cheap, reliable, lawn guy.

His paychecks will get larger. But I'd rather be poor and have him here with me.

I'll get sexy emails. But I'd prefer sexy time.

He and I will freeze time and the day he comes back it will be like he was never gone. But our daughters will be a year older, three inches taller, and he will NEVER be able to get that time back with them.

No one will steal my good candy. But I'll have no one to blame when I've eaten all my good candy.

I will be lonely. There is no "but". I will just be lonely. There will be a part of my heart that on every day of every week of every month of that year that will be empty. No friend, family member, activity, drink, or drug can fill it. Because they aren't him. He is the only thing that fits there.

Please don't let this be the time he's taken. Please let him come home. I know that I could do it without him, I just don't want to.

I love him.

Bipolar Check-in

please help me stay aware, so ask my #!

	Feels Like	Looks Like	What I need
1 Deep Depression	- Yoga pants & T's exclusively - A hole in my belly - It hurts to be alive. - SHAME -	- Consistently not answering phone. - Over eating - lethargic - sleeping a lot (not thyroid-related) - I actively push people away	- Don't want to talk. - Cuddling or being held - need to be around people, even if I'm in PJ's
2 Sad	- irritable - break plans to isolate - Feel very ashamed	- avoiding phone calls if possible. At a "2" I respond to calls w/ texts - pulling away - talk less - home more	- For people to understand how anxiety causing phones are in this state - Come to my house, encourage me to sit outside
3 even Keeled	feels great! Normal ups & downs but I can cope!	- Doing my best to answer calls & return them. - Like to do outings, museums, exercise - COOK!!	- Just my loved ones - Regular exercise - maintenance appts with my psychiatrist
4 Hypo-manic or mixed State	- Either feeling very happy & content or Anxious & sad * I will do all in my power to conceal #4 - Full of ideas. - Feels like there aren't reprocussions for decisions.	- I'm charasmatic & charming. - My speech is a bit faster - Buying things, lots of gift giving. - Lots of dating - desire to work out a lot. - Game face - I try to hide symptoms	* Non-Judgement on any/all of my behaviors * - "Noticing comments" - I notice you seem unusually happy. - Suggest I touch base w/ therapist (I might get mad.) because "4" feels good
5 Mania or psychotic break	- Feels like being high. - Out of control!! - Scary, exhilarating - Protective of mania - Psych. Break off feelings	- Pretty much focus is all about me. - Avoidance of established relationships & forming new superficial ones.	- Be calm & direct with your concerns - at the least asap appt with my psychiatrist - Maybe hospitalization

From the Artist:
"People always ask me about my son or my photography, but no one ever asks about my bipolar disorder. That is just as important... It took courage to make this chart. And that is why I ask my friends to please help me stay aware and ask my number!"

THERE ARE ALOT OF THINGS THAT **BULLY** ME. ONE IS MY MOST DISABLING ILLNESS. I AM BIPOLAR. THEY SAY YOU ARE NOT YOUR ILLNESS. BUT I THINK ITS A PART OF ME AT THIS POINT. THERE ISNOT A DAY I DO NOT HEAR ABOUT BIPOLAR BEING AN "EXCUSE" OR THE CAUSE OF ABUSE. WHETHER IT'S THE VOICES IN MY HEAD, OR THE GIRLS THE TABLE OVER IN THE CAFETERIA AT SCHOOL. I AM SO AFRAID. AFRAID THAT I WILL END UP LIKE THE REST.

I AM ALREADY DEFINED BY MY ILLNESS. THIS IS SCARIER THAN BEING TRANS, GENDERQUEER, QUEER OR BEING ME. MY ILLNESS IS NOT RESPONDING TO TREATMENT. I DON'T KNOW IF I CAN ACTUALLY LIVE ANYMORE. I IMAGINE LIVING IN AN ASYLUM FOR THE REST OF MY LIFE.

I am bi-polar. Whatever that means. I was self-medicating for a long time. I've been taking pills forever. They're gone now. I've spent ten years escaping from who I am, and now I am here to face me. And love me. Because my love has been everywhere; there is so much of it... but I forgot to learn to love myself. I thought I could be thinner, prettier, funnier, smarter.. to make myself fall in love with myself. But it didn't work! I saw right through all that.

i am weird
kids in high school hated me
so when i went to college, i started telling people
        that i was AUTISTIC
it's not true
but i told them that anyways

and suddenly
no longer was i a freak
there was a method to
        my MADNESS
i was brave
i was a survivor
i was a novelty
and i was popular

but when you're stuck in a lie
there's no getting out of it
especially when that lie gives you power

so the lies kept coming
i told people I was pregnant
        and then I told them I had a miscarriage
i made up boyfriends that didn't exist
i told people i was raped
i said i had cousins who died in 9/11
i even told 2 of my teachers i had cancer
        i even shaved my head

the real me is a high school fat bitch weirdo
        who ONLY wanted to be loved
but now the world sees a
        retarded rape and cancer victim
        trying to make her way in an unfair world

i should be shot!
i should be kicked!!
i should be stoned!!!

but you'd never stone a retard with cancer,
        would you? :-)

Sober 6, 5 years.
Still a junkie
Still an alkie
Still a failure
Still a fake

Silent. I am always silent. And when I'm not, I feel guilty. For things I have done, things I haven't, what I am, and what I try to be. Never enough. My family and "friends" agree (even if some refuse to admit it).

It hurts and sometimes I cry. I feel guilty for asking for help because I know someone is judging me — saying that I'm just seeking attention. Sometimes I want to wave goodbye, with a little less "good" and a lot more "bye". Sleep forever if I need to. But I know that I can't. Pounds of lead strapped to my leg and pulling my skin down. It hurts, but I feel weak if I cry. It hurts, but I feel guilty if I cry.

I AM SILENT

I STARTED SMOKING AT 12.

I STARTED DRINKING AT 13.

I STARTED SEX AT 14.

I FELT LOVE AT 15.

BUT ONLY TWO YEARS.

17 AND ALONE.

WHERE DO I GO FROM HERE?

a provided reality.

a   lonely   man   sits   in
a   lonely   room   and
writes   his   lonely   thoughts   to
make   you   laugh.

a stoplight interlude.

i never stop behind the white line. i bet those mongers at the dmv don't either. (they're human. i think.) i drum my fingers along the steering wheel to the new barenaked ladies song. i don't like it but it's catchy. too catchy. the gas station on the corner is empty and it should be. it's a cold and snowy tuesday night. and you pull up next to me. you capture my attention and squeeze. it's gotta be the cherry red pickup truck. i've always wanted one of those. i notice the fuzzy dice around your mirror. but you're not one of those people that have them there for show. (i can tell these things.) they mean something to you. i bet your boyfriend won them at some carnival on *the* perfectly romantic evening. (the one where you lost your virginity.) i can tell you're driving with a purpose. (i wish i was.) probably off to some coffee shop. not a starbucks though. one where all the smart and beautiful people go. your boyfriend will be there. i notice that you're singing along with the radio. my finger manipulates the tuner. i can't find the song to match your moist lips. maybe you're talking to yourself. planning what you're going to say to him. writing beautiful poetry. (i wish i was.) the barenaked ladies finally fade and the dj makes a feeble attempt at humor. (i imagine myself stabbing him to death. haha.)

the light turns green. (things aren't supposed to end with a green light.) i continue to drive. drumming my fingers. without a purpose.

Boy or girl — why.
WHY. WHY
CAN'T I JUST
BE A PERSON? STOP

"You would
be adorable
being a girl"

"You're being
the old you"

STOP STOP
STOP STOP STOP
STOP

People think, say, wonder

"What's wrong?" "I don't
Understand!"
"Are you sure?"

"Why don't
you try?"

Neutrois Aromantic
Asexual — what the hell.
Am I now an amoeba?
Transgender is **not**
transsexual — non-binary
people exist too.

I EXIST

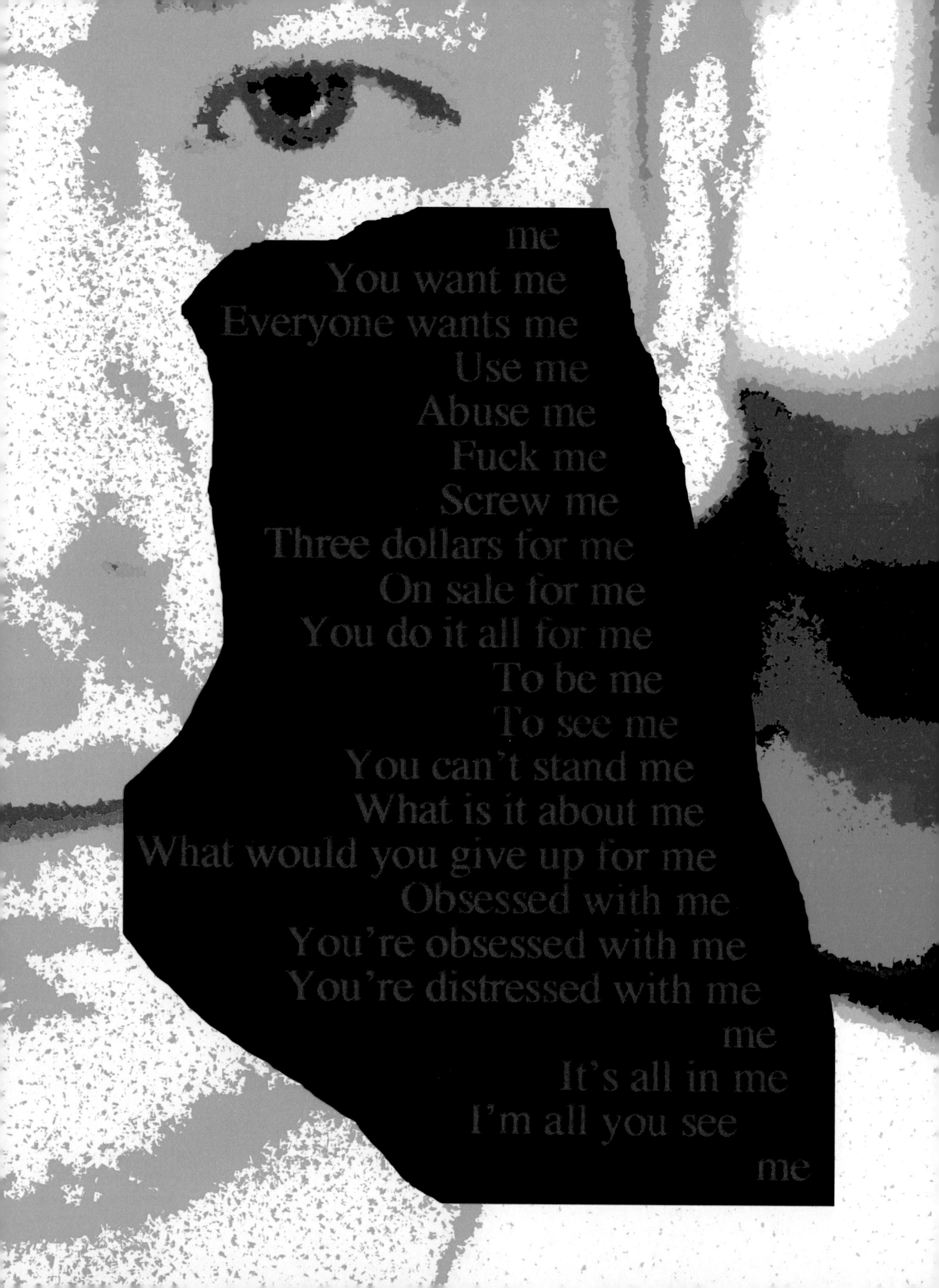

me
You want me
Everyone wants me
Use me
Abuse me
Fuck me
Screw me
Three dollars for me
On sale for me
You do it all for me
To be me
To see me
You can't stand me
What is it about me
What would you give up for me
Obsessed with me
You're obsessed with me
You're distressed with me
me
It's all in me
I'm all you see
me

It prospers
and it burns
into flames of the ocean
shallow rocks of the sea

they hit
they help,
      the waves from crashing my home,
           my land.

I prosper
   but, I burn

It get different
   things gett## [better]

   I will wait out the change
      as the waves are different
           day by
              day

I DRINK
SO I CAN THINK
BUT WHEN I THINK
I GET TIRED.

MAYBE IT'S THE MEDS
OR THE WARMTH OF MY BED
OR THE DEMONS IN MY HEAD
OR THE FACT THAT YOU THINK I'M A LIAR?

THE MOTIONS
AND EMOTIONS
ROLL THROUGH ME LIKE THE OCEAN
AND SET MY SOUL ON FIRE.

FOR WATER, FLAMES ARE NO MATCH
THEY FIZZLE AND SCRATCH
THEY ARE NO MATCH
COULD YOU, TOO, CALL THEM A ~~LIAR~~ LIAR?

TO YOU
I SPOKE TRUE
WITH WORDS BLACK AND BLUE
FROM A HEART DISSOLVING, DISAPPEARING INTO DARK.

BUT YOU TOOK
MY SECOND GLANCE, MY EMPTY LOOK
OH, HOW MY BROKEN SOUL SHOOK
THAT I WAS GLAD WE'D GROWN APART.

I AM NO LIAR.
I AM FOREVER ON FIRE.

Dear Ex-Boyfriend,

Let's have a real conversation, OK? Me and you. Just the 2 of us. We haven't talked since you dumped ~~me~~. Without reason or warning. It's been 8 years last February but I still ~~feel~~ you HERE next to me.

Don't worry, I've moved on. I'm in love! I think? It's diffrent, but it's real & right. I've ~~been~~ grown up. I don't get butterflies. I don't get giddy. I don't feel the rush of passion Like I once did with you. I am a different woman now. If you saw me on the street, you'd probably walk right by me. I'd notice you. My stomach would drop. I'd feel that rsssssssh. but you'd go unphased & pass me by as if I were a stranger.

I have ????'s. ~~Since~~ I've got your attention here, would you mind answering some of them? you continued to call me after you left. WHY? Did you expect me to answer the phone? Be your friend? I begged you to stay with me & you walked. So, why the phone calls?

I've ~~been~~ seen you with .... HER. You think no one else knows what's going on. She has someone, you know? She's taken. Your just her latest trick. ~~I don't do you think~~ How does that make you feel? Second-rate? I know the feeling.

Then the trivial bullshit. Is she better in bed than me? Prettier than me? Smarter than me? A better person? A better friend? She's got your attention, so ~~I don't~~ there's got to be something there that I'm not seeing.

MOST IMPORTANTLY, Did you ever love me? I don't know why I ask or why I care, but I just do. The truth sets a person free! (I think.) Please seriously consider your response before answering & don't lie. You wont break me (again).

You already did that once & like I said, I've moved on. Or something like that.

Love, or something like that...
ME

I LEFT MY ABUSIVE EX- AND SHE KEPT EVERYTHING - THE MONEY I GAVE HER TO GET HER OUT OF DEBT, MY FURNITURE, MY SOUVENIRS, THE PRICELESS THINGS THAT MEANT SO MUCH TO ME & NOTHING TO HER. BUT I'M OKAY- I'M OKAY & THAT TERRIFIES ME FOR SOME REASON.

"Dear" today: I <u>hate</u> you.   Please be <u>over</u>.
"Dear" universe, give me back my husband
I <u>thought</u> I was stronger than this.
But I applied for social security survivor
  benefits today   & it didn't <u>kill me</u>.
(My first <u>drink</u> of the day was before 9am.)
Merry <u>fucking</u> Christmas.

You should kill yourself because I hate you.
(I still want him)
              - my ex boyfriend of over a year.
                  also my first love.

HOT

Cock

INCOME

keep current on the always

PRIDE

Happiness

SIZE

FABULOUS

HIV care

HUSTLER

EXPERIENCE

BEING PROUD

BIRTHDAY

FIT

Things I'll never have.

Party!

Things I'll never be.

69

POSITIVE
IMAGES

MARRIAGE

EQUALITY

rentboy

HouseKeeper

ANNIVERSARIES

Production

From the Artist:
"I was recently diagnosed with multiple sclerosis and I also have AIDS. Not HIV but an actual AIDS diagnosis. I'm not near death, but I am far from healthy looking. Who wants to be with a man with a big belly and sunken cheeks and death pumping through his veins...? A hot body, hot boyfriend, more birthdays, a new car, sex, love, money, beauty, healthcare, my Mother's forgiveness. Those are the things I'll never have and the things I'll never be."

From the Artist:
"No matter how many weights I lift, no matter how big my pecs and biceps get, no matter how many pool parties I get invited to, no matter how many drugs I do... I am silently ashamed of who I have become. I am 54 and I've never been in love with anyone but myself."

←LIES

From the Artist:
"We'd been together for over a decade. I told him I wanted to get married. He said that marriage was "so sacred" to him that he wanted to wait until it was legal for us gays. For him, "a civil union simply would not do."
Well, gay marriage became legal in our state in June of 2013... and then he dumped me in July. Always a groomsmen, Never a groom... & now forever alone."

Just because I'm TRANS doesn't mean I'll fuck you.
'Cuz I still have a DICK doesn't mean I'll suck you.
Because you call me a FREAK doesn't mean I'm freaky in the sheets
SHUT UP!
'Cuz I'm busy $AVING up for my new VAGINA.

<u>What are you $AVING up for, BITCH?!</u>

I breathe, therefore I am
But not what people tell me I am
Smash the Cis-tem!!!
Break the glass walls
Because we can see through them
So let us through, already
we're breaking down the closet doors
and the closet walls
there's no monsters in the closet
Where is this damn closet anyway?

From the Artist:
"I never intend to offend when I transgender-bend!"

From the Artist:
"Just because I don't believe in God
doesn't mean that I am not a good person.
I could go on for days, trying to defend my Atheism --
but there's no point. Either you embrace religious freedom
and rational thinking or you don't. It's not my job to
convince you to be open minded. I have no desire to waste
my breath or beliefs on the ignorant and uninformed."

"Footprints in the sand are sedimentary
Proof of Your Existence...

                        ...but I haven't been to the beach in years.
I spend my days ambling
                down
                    the concrete sidewalks of
                         West Hollywood,
Each step leaving no trace of where I've been or sign of where
I'm going.
        It's like chasing pavement with manmade anonymity.

BUT...
        There is NO question You Exist: Live, Thrive, forever Alive.

My life has been filled with far too many seemingly happenstance
        coincidences for them to have been engineered
                      by Chance."

My husband carries around a prescription bottle of Viagra in his brief case. He says it's because he likes to jerk off in his office, but I know it's because he's cheating on me.

I think it's sad what he is doing but, but what I think is sadder is that I no longer care. We have been married 11 years and I will get half of everything.

Who's a FUCK UP?
I'M a FUCK UP!
Just ask my Dad.
He'll tell you.
I'M a FUCK UP!
When we're alone He tells me that if I don't stop FUCKING UP he'll FUCK ME UP.
He uses his fists to make me a better person.
I am thankful.
I'M a FUCK UP!
However black, blue and broken bones will be my salvation.
I AM a FUCK UP!

How many times can a heart break before it stops working? The answer is seven. How do I know this? I recently had my seventh miscarriage. From this. I will never recover, It is over for us. I will never recover and I don't think my marriage will either.

I am lonely because my family is different from most. They think I am garbage.

I was born into a family that pretended to love me because they felt they had to, but then I grew up and made a new family who loves me because they want to. I miss my mother and father and brother but living an authentic life is more important to me than having pretend love. I only wish I didn't have to choose.

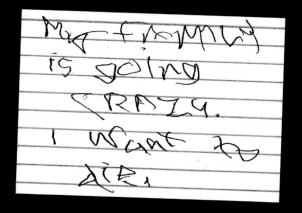

My FAMILY is going CRAZY. I want to die.

When I was a little boy, my mother used to let out her anger at me. This lasted until I turned 20 years old.

At first it was the state that separated me from my dad. He would overdose, I'd get put in foster care, he'd get sober and work to get me back, things would be fine for a bit, then he'd overdose again and the cycle would repeat itself... But one day, it wasn't the state that took him away. He simply disappeared. Days turned into weeks. Weeks turned into months. He was gone this time, really gone -- and this time he left on his own free will. I pretended I didn't care, but it hurt so much. So I wrote him this letter and sent it to the last known address I had for him:

TO DAD:
1. My best friend that I cannot live without
2. Dance. To let my emotions out
3. I did my first pageant
4. I finally started my career
5. I am a leader, to show that life is worth it
6. I went to prom with a guy I think I love
7. I am going to be ok

These are the things you have missed since you have been gone.

He found me on Facebook and wrote back:

and your point is? leave me alone............ I will get a restraining order on you if you contact me again......... you tell this shit........ to someone who cares........blocked

I haven't seen my father since.

From the Photographer:
"I pass this every day on my morning hike. You probably wouldn't even notice it, but I do because I miss my Dad too. He killed himself and didn't leave a note... I guess he had other things on his mind."

From the Photographer:
"My father drinks out of the toilet, straight Patron alone in the bathroom. He thinks it's less degrading than having us watch him get plastered in the living room...but my father is wrong. Our whole fucking life is pathetic! And my worst fear is that I'll start drinking out of the toilet soon too. You know what they say... Like father, like son.

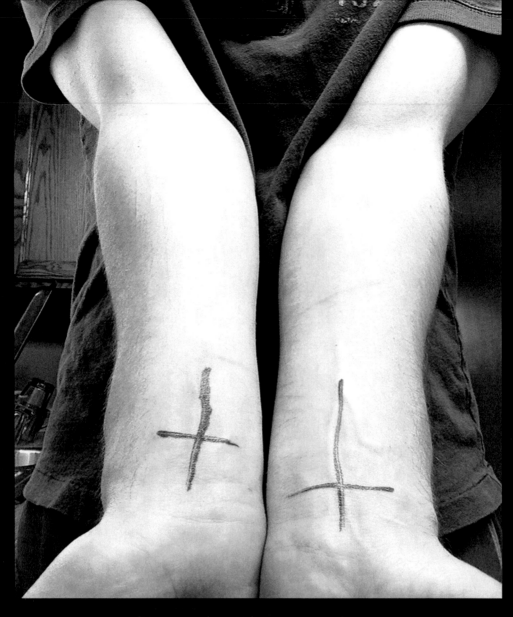

From the Photographer:
"The upside down crosses are only for shock value. Don't worry.
I'm not a Satanist. At least I don't think I am. At least not yet.
No... What should really concern you are the scars on my arms.
Mostly healed, almost invisible, but each cut deliberate, the deep
red of the blood making me feel like I'm alive, like I have some
sort of control in this fucked up world! Why am I such a mess?
Take your pick. My daddy left. My mom's a drunk. The neighbor
fucked me when I was 14. I drink cold medicine for breakfast and
I shoot cooked up household cleaners into my veins...! Or maybe
none of this is true and I'm just fucking with you. Maybe
manipulation is how I maintain some sort of control of the idiots
in my shit-ass life. Maybe. Or maybe all of this IS true. Maybe."

clichéd Endings

My sister's father died today
(he deserved it)
Through my empty eyes and listless
emotions, I can only express one thought
(minus silent rejoicings)
Should I wear black
(how cliché)

Please teach me how to speak...
And not hate myself.

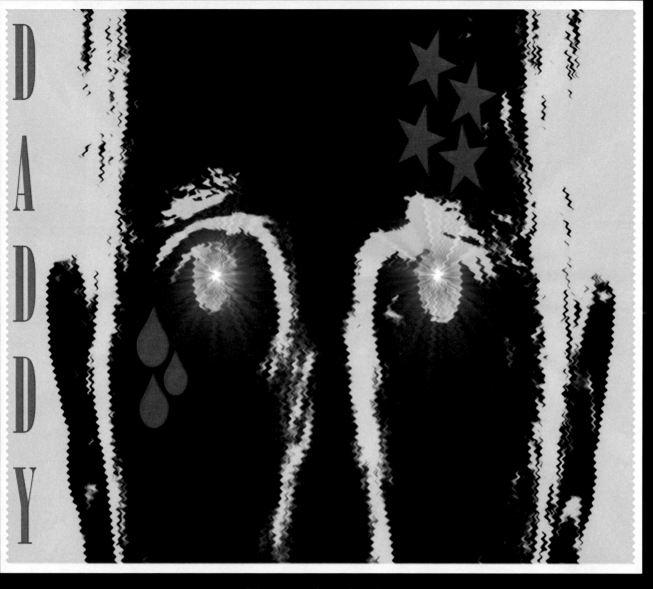

From the Artist:

"I was 13 when someone told me what Daddy's teardrops meant. I didn't believe them until I asked my mother... She never verbally confirmed he was a killer, but the way she sobbed and shook was confirmation enough... Because my father was incarcerated for much of my childhood, I never knew him. But once he got out, we became acquainted -- not as father/daughter but as friends. Who I got to know was a kind and gentle man who had learned from his mistakes and wanted to give back... At age 63, my father had 4 stars tattooed atop his eye. He said that this was to counteract the teardrops and represent the lives he had saved through his work as a reformed women's anti-violence advocate... You can never change the mistakes in your past, but you can help make the world a better place when you choose to live in love."

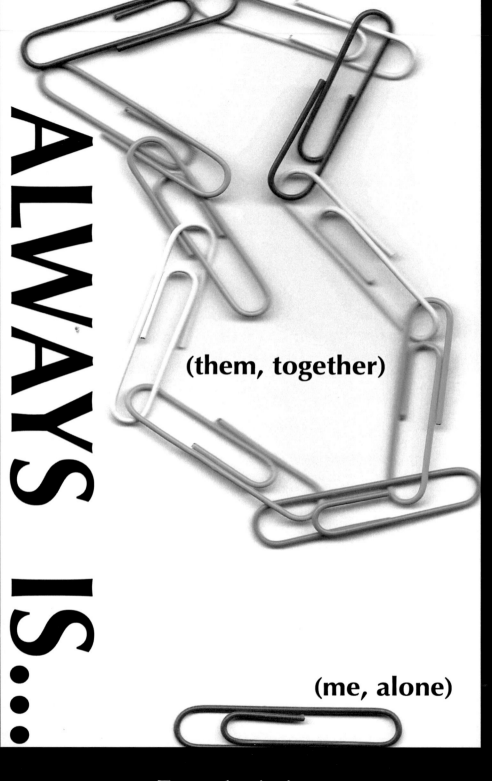

ALWAYS IS...

(them, together)

(me, alone)

From the Artist:
"From the outside looking in, always on the outside
looking in. Being so self-aware is exhausting."

how i spend my life.

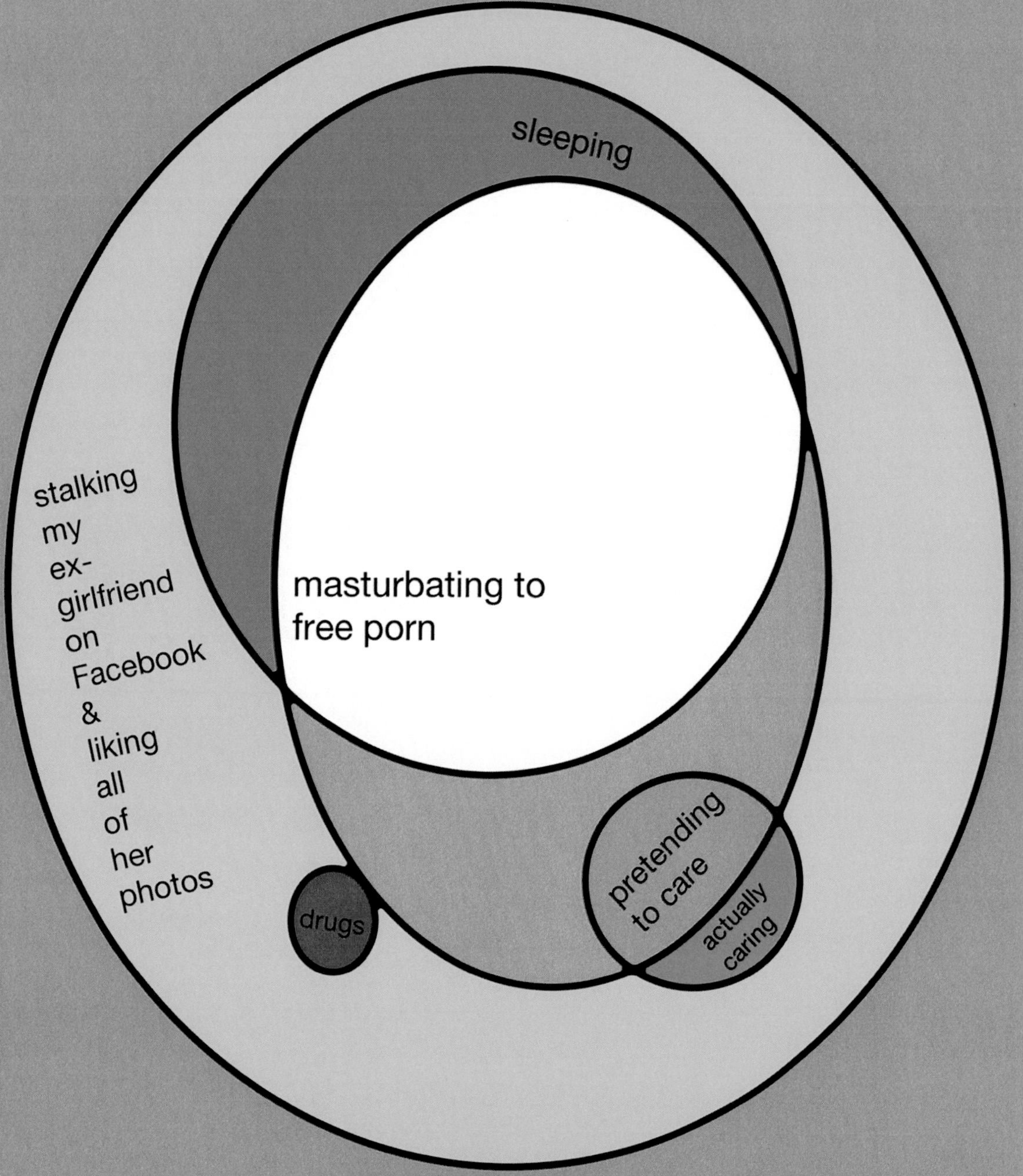

sleeping

stalking
my
ex-
girlfriend
on
Facebook
&
liking
all
of
her
photos

masturbating to
free porn

drugs

pretending
to care

actually
caring

i am 32 and i still live with my parents.

Thankyou!
& know you're Beautiful!!!

```
                     Bar
                     Blvd
               Hollywood, Ca

Server:                      2014
Table 13/1              8:19 PM
Guests: 2                  80061

Bacardi                       8.00
Margarita (2 @9.00)          18.00
Lamb Chops (2 @15.00)        30.00
Dbl Fed Wing                 16.00
Brussel\nSprout               7.00

Subtotal                     79.00

Tax Exclusive Tax             7.11

Total Tax                     7.11

Total                        86.10

Balance Due        86.10

      Checks split 4 ways per table.
         Suggested Gratuity:
            18% = 14.22
            20% = 15.80
                      bar.com
      facebook.com/          bar
```

"My boyfriend drinks too much, but so do I. Perhaps that's why we're such a great pair... Recently, we went out to dinner. We both got raging drunk. (We showed up drunk and only drank more as we ate.) Things got a little nasty (which they usually do when we drink), and he started screaming that I've gotten "too fat and ugly to fuck!" The waitress was horrified and stopped coming to our table... When the check eventually came, she handed it to me with the kindest of eyes. She squeezed my hand and walked away, saying nothing. I opened up the check and saw what she had written at the top... I save this receipt in my purse because it makes me smile. No one has ever called me beautiful before."

From the Artist:
"This will sound disgusting. I even cringe as I write it...but my vagina is not normal. The best way to describe it? It's like a bomb went off in it. It's not clean and tucked like the women you see in magazines or in porn videos. The lips look almost like a wilting orchid flower or a wet weeping willow. They just sort of hang there, and it makes me feel like a broken, disgusting woman. My boyfriend agrees. Sometimes after sex, he calls me "Meat Flaps" or "The Exploding Clam" or a "Wet & Flabby Taco." I pretend to laugh but I die a little inside... I hate him. I hate my body. I hate myself. I hate sex. I hate my Meat Flaps."

A party with friends on New Year's Eve. Who doesn't want to do that? If I could take one night back as a do-over it would be this one. A night of socializing with friends turned into one of my biggest regrets. I should have stayed home to watch Dick Clark on TV and to see that fucking ball drop one more time. The ball sure did drop that year for me and it has taken me nearly 20 years to work through things — although I don't know if one ever really can. Drinking and games is all well and good until that one outside guy friend's decides to fucking take you into your dad's office to rape you. This guy looked like a prick. I wouldn't give him a kiss on the cheek at New Year's — as a result he literately "fucked" me up — emotionally and physically. I snuck out of the house after everyone slept. My friends stopped talking to me (which it took me years to understand that this was due to their being cowards and nothing to do with me). I played things off like everything was okay. I wasn't okay. I wasn't for a long time. I ate a lot to hide my pain. I got fat. I became depressed. I felt alone.

I felt undeserving of love. I was ashamed
for being too trusting. I protected my
family instead of myself. I had no
courage to seek this jackass down and
put him in jail. One night and
everything changed. Nothing felt right.
I ~~no~~ longer knew who I was.
Somehow I found strength and have
seen past this, but I have lived a life
alone still feeling as though I am
undeserving of love. I wanted the house,
kids, a big family. I often wonder if
now it's too late. I've never really enjoyed
New Year's Eve since. I doubt that I ever will.

THE WOUND IS THE PLACE WHERE THE LIGHT ENTERS YOU.
—Rumi

From the Artist:
"Growing up, whenever I was upset I would draw...but my mom got sick and I was told that there was no time for drawing anymore. Then my father got sick. Then my brother got sick, really sick. And then my sister got sick too. Through all of that, I never drew. Fifteen years went by and I never drew a single thing...but this week I picked up a pencil and this came out of me. I think I'll start drawing again."

From the Artist:
"This is me. This is a self-portrait... I spent my whole life thinking I was ugly. My childhood, my teens, even through my 30s, not a single day went by when I didn't feel ugly. I knew I was a good artist but that is all I was -- an ugly girl that was good at art. It took getting cancer, treating my cancer and beating cancer for me to realize that I am beautiful. There is a reason I am still here... This is me and I am beautiful."

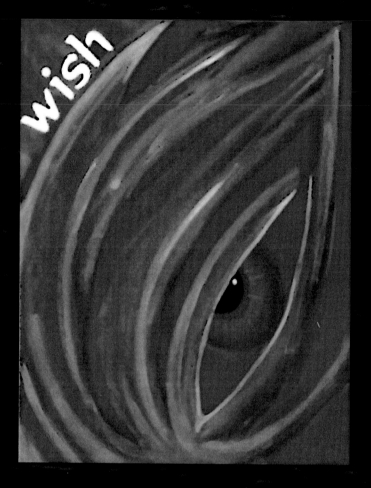

wish

From the Artist:
"When I created this, I was going through a lot of emotional pain -- anything and everything in regards to finances and long-term relationship issues. But when I am feeling emotionally overloaded and enough is enough, I let my TEARS start to flow. I let loose onto the canvas! In that moment, life feels like it's about to end but my tears help me open up... and the answers eventually come."

From the Artist:
"For much of my life, I have felt that my identity was fragmented and I had difficulty knowing exactly who I was. It felt like I had too many sharp edges and contrasting colors to ever make a cohesive whole. It has only been in the past few months that I have started fitting all of the pieces together. What has resulted may not come together seamlessly...but it is beautiful and it is me. I am good enough."

From the Artist:
"I am a woman who is constantly discriminated against daily because I am BUTCH. I have been mistaken for a male time after time. In the workplace or public, people see what they want to see and not what's really in front of them... People should stop assuming and judging a book by its cover and instead take the time to get to know each other -- regardless of race, color, religion or sexual orientation."

From the Artist:
"I have struggled with an eating disorder since I was 14 years old... For years I was in denial, even as I nearly starved myself to death. It was only in my 20's that I admitted I had a problem. Now as I fight it, the disorder feels overwhelming. Sometimes it seems to be pulling me in, forcing lies out of my mouth and digging its clawed fingers into my brain... Recovery is hard so there are days when I feel like drawing. Drawing it lets me put it on paper instead of letting it fester inside of me."

From Da'Coata, the injured puppy:
"My Daddy took me to the pet spa, but it was horrible! They locked me in a cage for 4 hours alone. I hurt my neck and tore open all of my paws; I spent two days in the hospital! My Daddy complained to the manager, and this is what he wrote:

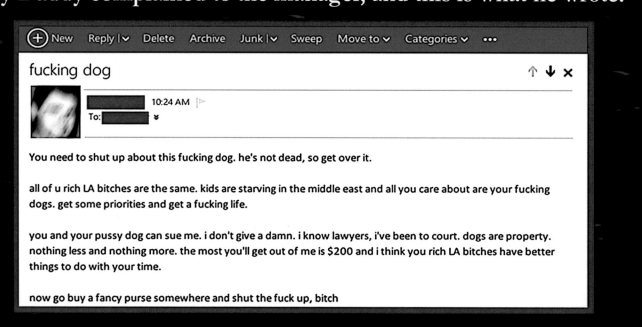

New   Reply | ⌄   Delete   Archive   Junk | ⌄   Sweep   Move to ⌄   Categories ⌄   •••

fucking dog   ↑ ↓ ✕

10:24 AM
To:

You need to shut up about this fucking dog. he's not dead, so get over it.

all of u rich LA bitches are the same. kids are starving in the middle east and all you care about are your fucking dogs. get some priorities and get a fucking life.

you and your pussy dog can sue me. i don't give a damn. i know lawyers, i've been to court. dogs are property. nothing less and nothing more. the most you'll get out of me is $200 and i think you rich LA bitches have better things to do with your time.

now go buy a fancy purse somewhere and shut the fuck up, bitch

A month later, a kitten died at the same spa. My Daddy feels responsible and can't forgive himself for not doing more."

People who hate Animals...

Bully me!!!

My 4-year-old dog unexpectedly, without warning, <u>DIED</u> last night.
<u>BLOAT</u>, the doctors say! (My previous dog died from the same thing).
I have been screaming and hysterically crying since 1:00 AM.
It's my fault. During our walk yesterday, I let a stranger sitting outside in a cafe feed him a piece of chicken as we walked by.
Who lets their baby take food from a stranger? I am a horrible mother. I should be shot, stabbed, charged, jailed, <u>KILLED!</u>
He was my buddy and my best friend. I <u>LOVED</u> him.
<u>IN SHOCK!</u> I WANT TO DIE! <u>HELP ME!</u>

From the Photographer:
"When my boyfriend asked me to take an Alaskan cruise with him, I was pleasantly surprised. I thought we were on the verge of breaking up, but I took his invite as a sign that we were doing better... I couldn't have been more wrong! It turns out he had been cheating on me for the past year with a mutual friend. He thought I deserved to hear it from him directly, and he wanted to tell me somewhere where I "wouldn't make a scene and couldn't run away." I guess he thought that a cruise ship in the middle of the ocean was the perfect place to tell me he was an asshole...!

I spent the whole trip crying. I slept in hallways, didn't go on any excursions, avoided all activities and other people. I allowed my heartbreak to isolate me from everything and everyone... It wasn't until months later (after we'd gotten back and I had moved out) that I began looking through the photos I had listlessly taken. It was the first time I had noticed the awe-inspiring splendor that had surrounded me. It was through my photographs that I realized how insignificant life's small heartaches truly are. I felt this inexplicable emotional release of sorts, but I also felt so cheated! Why had I not allowed myself to see such beauty?! But I don't blame myself. Us human beings are conditioned to live in our problems and not life's beauty. But I now love myself enough to stop that insidious cycle and embrace all I've been given... even $5,000 cruises from a each-hole!"

From the Photographer:
"My boyfriend and I have been dating for 14 months, but he still makes me climb out of this window every time his ex-wife comes over. He doesn't want me to exit through the front door because she might see me and get "triggered." Now, I understand that they share 10 years of history, but I shouldn't be climbing out windows. Because that triggers ME...and yet he doesn't seem to care."

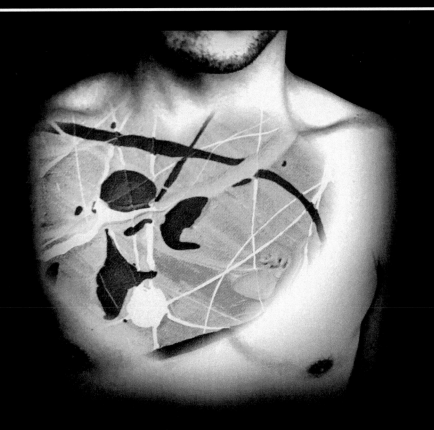

From the Artist:
"I don't like to focus on love like the rest of my generation does -- how we feel that if someone isn't dating us then there must be something wrong with us. It's as if love has become a poison, and the only cure is to tear ourselves apart in order to find something we aren't meant to find."

I
BULLY
ME
MOST OF
ALL!

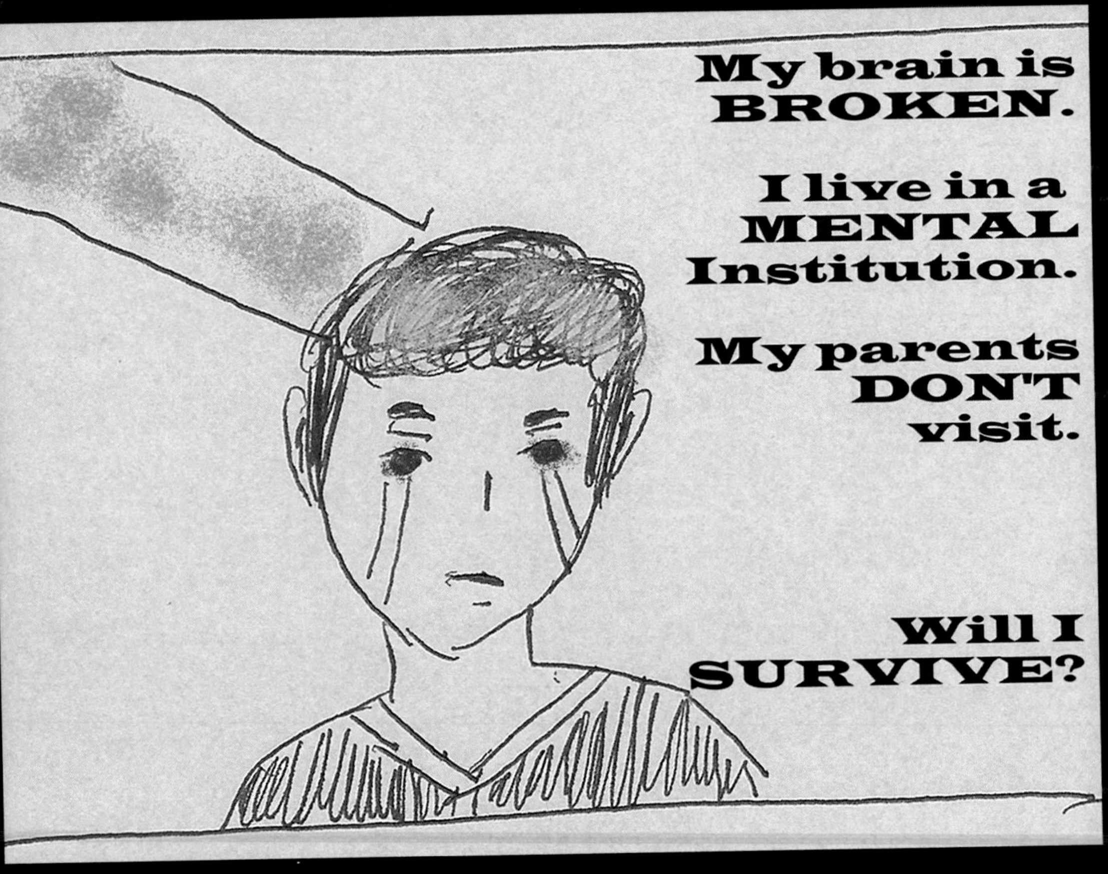
My brain is
BROKEN.
I live in a
MENTAL
Institution.
My parents
DON'T
visit.
Will I
SURVIVE?

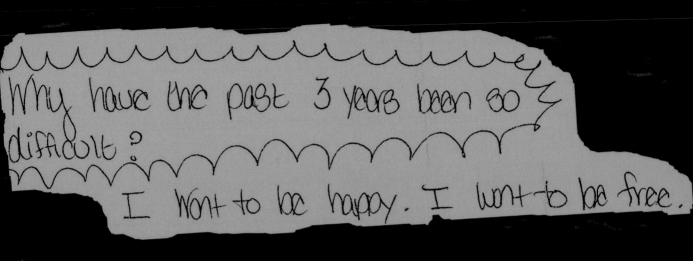

Why have the past 3 years been so difficult?

I wont to be happy. I wont to be free.

HOMOPHOB A.

(plain & simple.)

Scarred Skin & Tree Bark

Decisions, happenstance, encounters both random and coincidental; those are the things that make us who we are. But I truly do believe that it is a single moment that frames us with definition and enlivens our existence. The "we" that we were born to be -- our culture, our passion, the essence that makes the me a me -- comes to life in a singular, cellular-stirring second.

I have only been in love, true love, once; a hideously insidious experience -- not completely to the man I married, not to my first kiss, not the beautifully brave boy who brought me to his prom, nor the gentleman that once flew to Rome on a whim. Not like, not lust, but a holistic, soul and mystic love -- only once -- with the kind of connection that lands you in the loony bin after the honeymoon gives way to solitude.

The story of us -- the details of how we came to be and ultimately fell apart into a distant me and he -- read quite cliché. (But then again, don't they always?)

I do not blame him because I do not understand him; never will and, now I see, never have. He is famous; I am not. He is beautiful; I am not. He is magmatic, magnetic; I am not. And he is a child of god, an orphan in a spiritually alien world that I do not -- no, cannot, will not, shall not -- no, never comprehend.

He owns a cabin in the woods just outside of Sun Valley, Idaho -- his clandestine escape, tucked away so remote and deep that even his god not dare peer through the trees. I still have a key; and months after he released me, solitarily so back into the unknown, I broke in.

I stayed a week. Alone, finding beauty in fallen tree bark. And then I left, erasing any tracing of my time there -- as he had so artfully, so easily, far too eagerly done with me.

One year later, to the exact date and time, I came back. I do not know why; but then again, what's the use in asking why? For introspective, self-reflective unanswered queries forever leaves one hollow, drains the marrow dry.

Standing beneath the gargoyled trees of grotesquely-knotted bark, shielded from a metaphoric heaven while grounded in the literal dirt of a dying earth, I

From the Author:
"No matter how hard I try, I don't think I'll ever get over my first love. It's been 15 years since we last spoke, and I still write about him all the time. Some of the stories are based in truth and others are purely fictitious longings about the love that got away; this one is a combination of both. But does it really matter? No, it doesn't...because whatever I write, the goal remains the same. I want him to read it and come back home."

made a resolution -- to return to this home, year after year, each time alone. Why? I do not know. To connect, reflect on a retrospect that had long ago died? Does it even matter?

Because I continued to return. For years; six of them, in fact. A fantastic, concentric, sadistic ritual of elective loneness... until my seventh showing.

Because this time, he was there.

I'd like to think it was happenstance, an encounter both random and coincidental -- but I assume rather, a neighbor had told him that a strange man, the shell of a wayward sentinel, was allowing himself (myself) in, uninvited, each and every February Twenty-Fourth with a once-given but long-forgotten key.

There, he stood. Here, I stood. Where we stood? I do not know.

We didn't speak, but we made dinner. We didn't speak, but we drank wine. We didn't speak, but we sat on the porch in chairs that his grandfather had once fashioned by calloused, god-fearing hands out of fallen tree bark. Not once did we speak... but twice we made love.

I accepted his silence because I knew that he believed that if the "we" that we were being went unacknowledged and unspoken then it didn't exist; it wouldn't matter if god took a gander through those tall and twisted trees, his gaze breaking through bark big and coarse. Because we had invented a new undecipherable language, elevated and without code, the intimations of a brave and reborn semi-queer race that spoke only through sensory pleasure and unbreakable stares with his baby blue eyes.

The food, the wine, the porch, the tears, the release, the warmth, a godliness neither of us had ever known; salvation in the form of skin and tissue as scarred as broken bark. But this time not alone.

That night rushed forth at a clip far too quick -- so fast, in fact, that I sometimes swore gravity had lost its penchant to pull downward and instead thrown life, time and space into an inexplicable fast-forward -- in a stillness and silence who's antithesis has long come to define me.

He drifted to sleep in my arms, arms weak with need, arms feeble in grasp. Because those arms awoke in an empty bed, a cabin still, an abandoned hideaway under godless watch. He was gone; no note, no sign, no baby blues to release me solitarily so back into the unknown; artfully, easily, eagerly, again swept aside. Alone.

I spent the day in a rental car -- waiting for what, I do not know; perched on the shoulder of a less-traveled road, the only passage into our clandestine world, scripting unreal and ultimately unrealized opportunity with each anonymous set of passing headlights, and surrounded by the beauty of fallen bark that had, in one night, grown dry with time.

They make fun of
my eyebrows. I have
No real friends.

Right now I feel like I dont know myself I have a thing called Aleopisa (I lose my hair) I feel like my worlds crashing down because my hair was my identity..What people see when they look at me, People try and understand but they cant. I feel like Im loosing myself and who I am. I try so hard to be positive but everytime I get happy it overpowers me with sadness. This is one of my bad days...I cant stop crying and im not focessed. I know my hair isn't everything that makes me, me, but it still hurts.

HONEST FEELINGS

From: ████████████████████ (an Oscar-winning actress)
Sent: Mon 6/17/13 10:09 AM
To: writtenbyanonymous@live.com

```
my face
my body
my hair
my eyes
even my fucking teeth
are not my own.
I look in the mirror and see a product and it really fuckin sucks to
not have control over who you are. what you are. something as
personal as the way u look.
does this make any sense?
starting in this business all i wanted was to be pretty. as pretty as
they come. sit me in that hair/make-up chair all damn day if you have
to and brush away the lines and bleach their hair until every woman
wants to be ME and every man wants to fuck me!
and its good. for a while.
but then they decide you should have red hair
new teeth
lose weight.
then gain weight and have "them" talk about you being pregnant.
[they even started a rumor that i bleached my anus. um, i
meannnnnnnn!]
and also to date men. always men. alwys more and more men. boring
men. men that like my hair and nothing more. the hair that is not my
own.

u can probably fit 500 people in my house, but u know what? NO ONE
COMES OVER. ever. and not because im a lonely loser, but because i'm
never theree.
and truthfully, its not even my house. I only put 3% down because
THEY tell me i need to move every few years.
seriously, it's not even only the way i look but they decide where i
live TOO.

and what's wrong with YOU?
why would YOU care? watch the shows? read the magazines? BUY the
magazines? click on the websites. Do you really honestly care what
color my hair is? who im fucking? where im living? how much i'm
drinking?
[i drink every night, BTW. vodka. rocks. a lot.]

"THEY" say it masks the pain and THEYre probably right, but i'm so
used to wearing masks so what's one more?
```

██████████████ (activist & non-profit president)
March 25

Monday Rant:
I have a disability. I require of government assistance to pay for caregivers to help me in my home, to live independently– I don't like it but that's just how it is. There are many people on such assistance...(along with others who abuse the system).
Sooo...when I go into the office to drop off documents that "prove" me eligible to receive such services, I expect long lines and crabby case workers. I expect to have to explain myself. That's fine. Ok.
I do not expect to be treated like dirt and spoken to in a condescending manner. I expect that when I say "Thanks" or "Have a good day" I at least see a glimpse of acknowledgement that I spoke. I expect that I be allowed to speak and not cut off as soon as I open my mouth...
I look around and in this room filled with people looking for help (mental illness, unemployed, disabilities, etc.) everyone is being treated like garbage. Could it be that when someone is in need, YOU–bitter–and–horrible–human–being–of–a–case–worker, are just crushing spirits and contributing to all that is bad in the world?

Did your parents never teach you to treat others with dignity?

👍 79 💬 27

Unlike · Comment · Share

My mother used to tell me that telling a lie is how the devil takes over your soul. Well I lie all the time. Does that make me a member of satan's army? worse than that is it bad that I don't care? People come + People go, but I'm the one who puts on the show. Liar, Liar, my pants are on fire! and it feels goooooooooooooooooood!!!!!!!!!!!!!!!!!!!!!!!!!!

Right now I feel like I am on the outside looking in at the rest of the world. Outside is where, I don't know. All I know is that I feel cold and alone. I am adopted. That is kind of an excuse of a statement to make. "I am adopted and therefore I feel alone." It's cliché maybe even in some people's books. However, there is truth behind it. I understand my life is probably better than it would have been had I not been given up for adoption. It is weird to me, though, to look around and know that the blood running through the veins of my "family" is not identical to mine. I put quotes around "family" not meaning I don't love them, but they are not my traditional birth-right family. They are my loving family. I love them and the quotes mean no disrespect. I am just trying to distinguish what I mean for all of you who don't understand. If you're not adopted, you wouldn't understand. Don't look at my aloneness with pity or judgement please. I do try to fit in. I smile more than anyone else I know. ☺ But I tell you that something in me DID break the day my (non-quotes) family let me go. Even if I find them I will never be complete, and I am and will always feel like part of me is on the outside looking in at the rest of the world.

I feel this way right now, and I feel this way everyday. But I smile more than anyone else I know. ☺

This moment. I'm scared. I don't know whats in the future. I sit at school. stare at the clock and wait for the bell to ring. To have no responsibility. I move tomorrow. I move into foster care. I leave the place that sculpted who I was. I leave behind a girl who I can't leave, a girl who has sculpted who I am. my bestfriend. I leave the water balloon fiants & the random baking sessions. I leave my home. The same home where I see flashbacks. Flashbacks of my dad hitting me. My brother fondling me around. I see a police officer making me break by calling me a peice of shit. The flashback and memories of my father. Trying to die. Murder himself. A guy that overdosed 3 times. I hear his voice echo in my head. the voice of overdose. I've been hurt, and I love the house that built me but I hate this house, that makes me terrified. I see the chain I wanted to hang myself with... dangling. the memory. I go into foster care tomorrow. I see nothing front of me. I don't know. Sometimes I want to sit in a corner, feel invisible, so I don't get seen. I don't get hurt. His voice. The smack of the belt. I will walk out tomorrow with my bags in hand. I'm leaving this house, that tore me into peices. But, this moment. Is yet so far away. His voice. Help me. Foster care.

Social Media's
Ideal Woman.
Perfect Body
Perfect HAIR
Perfect boyfriend
PERfect Life.
No FLAWS

My husband
wants a divorce.
He says I've
gotten old + fat.
Fuck him! And the
23 year old whore
he's fucking.

The first time I remember hating my body
I was 4 years old. I was at a friends house.
We just picked apples off the tree + sat down
at the picnic table to eat them. I noticed
that when I sat down my thighs spread a
bit. I was so ashamed. After years of
battling my weight (I was a thin 4 yr old though
+ years of counseling I find my self
holding a pillow or purse on my lap when
I sit down. Even now I don't want to
have to look at my thighs. I'm in my 30's
for Christ's sake. I get anxious thinking
about warmer seasons because I can't
cover my body in a long coat. I need to
lose 100 pounds. Even if I do, the
4 year old inside of me will surely
still hate her thighs.

My loan for undergrad was $55,000 I only needed to take $47,000 but "WHY NOT?!" take the extra $8,000 for "fun money", right?!

My loan for grad school was $68,000. I only needed to take $51,000 but "WHY NOT?!" take the extra $17,000 for "A LOT of fun money", right?!

Now I have an MBA and also work nights at TGI Fridays and I will until I am dead.

#drowningindebt

I feel like this pressure drives my life to do better, be better, be the best possible person I can be, but it's stress. It's Stressing Me Out!

The bullies from high school never went away in my head - 40 years. 5 men have loved me, - (more than most people experience!!) really loved me - from 14 years old (really 10 yrs) - a teacher through my current boy friend. But I never feel attractive and never feel worthy.

In fact, today is my 5 year anniversary of sorts. I tried to kill myself 5 years ago today. Virtually no one knows it. Not my extended family - not my closest friends. But I know it. And I fight it - every day. Sometimes. As you said, sometimes it gets better - And sometimes it doesn't. But you go on.

My free SPIRIT is Hidden in caves OF F.E.A.R. & not belonging.

I do not have someone that loves me this much. For me high school is not a happy time. I can honestly say that I do not have one real friend. I have friends but they do not know me at all. They do not know the real me. The same for my family and at my job and at my church. I feel like I need to be a certain type of person in order for them to accept me.

But I am not that person. And the more I try to be that person, the more I slowly disappear. And the worst part is that no one seems to notice. Its as if everyone would rather have me quiet and in the corner and supposedly normal instead of love me for who I am.

I always thought I had a lot to offer. I always thought that I saw the world in a different way and that it was a better way. But by the way everyone around me acts (and wants me to act), it seems that I might just be wrong. I might not be special. At least special in the good meaning of the word. I might just be a problem that's meant to be fixed. Not a person that is meant to be loved yet. And now after years of feeling this way deep inside, I truly feel that they may be right.

I stand in my own way. I talk myself out of things I should do.

And it's sickening to me. I know my potential I know my capabilities. Why do I continue to cripple myself?

I think back to that 10-yr old child. Alone, scared, terribly shy and isolated. Staring, big-eyed, please see me? Help me?

The wake up call. "Why do you have a tummy ache every day?" Why, indeed.

I see her now. I embrace her. A tight, enveloping, accepting hug. Look at me now, I tell her. It's gonna be okay. You'll get there!

She shut down. All those years. Can't blame her, it was best that she did that.

But now -- time to open up! It's definitely time. I'm ready to be open, vulnerable, exposed. It feels good.

She looks up at me with her big eyes. Yes, she says, it's safe now. Thank you for coming back for me.

Two Wolves

There once was a young man all of sixteen years. On the outside, he appeared like everyone else; however, inside there raged an emotional war that he could not understand. For years, he kept his confusion to himself, living in a world of silence wrapped in shame. But one day that raging war became too much to handle; and for no reason in particular, something inside the boy broke open. He needed to know -- *What is the force inside of me that's pulling me apart?!*

So the young man turned to the only person he knew he could trust -- an art teacher at his high school with whom he felt a strong kinship. He asked his teacher for insight into the shameful war that raged within him. The teacher responded with a knowing and non-shaming smile, for he understood these feelings all too well.

"The way I see it," the art teacher said, *"there are two wolves that live inside of us. On the outside, both of them appear physically beautiful, inviting and sweet. However, their souls are quite different."*

He continued: *"One of them lives in a world of self-doubt. He is an angry, scared and boastful wolf. He hides behind a fur coat that stands on edge with confusion, insecurity and self-loathing, which leaves him forever lonely. This wolf hates himself and despises anyone who dares try to care for him."*

"But then there is the second wolf," smiled the teacher. *"He lives in a world of beauty -- not because the world is always beautiful, but because he chooses to focus on the good that comes his way. He is a loving and kind wolf; and while his heart sometimes gets hurt, he remains open to all those he encounters. He believes in second chances, resiliency and the promise of each new day. This wolf loves himself and all those that cross his path. This wolf is pure good."*

The boy nodded, as art teacher went on: *"As we grow, these wolves battle for dominance and control. Because although they may try, they cannot live side by side. In order for one to survive, the other must die. And that is the turmoil you feel inside."*

After a long pause, the boy looked up. He finally understood the war the raged within him, for it was the battle between self-love and self-hate. But with that realization came confusion, and so the boy asked: *"But if they cannot live together...which wolf wins?"*

The art teacher responded: *"The one you feed."*

RITE YOUR LETTE

UNPLUG. Turn off your cell phone, put the kids to bed and log off Facebook. Pour yourself a good glass of wine or make a fresh cup of coffee. If you're gonna do this correctly, you're gonna need "me, myself and only I" time.

FIND A SHEET OF PAPER. Any type, any size, anything goes.

ASK YOURSELF the question: *What is it that bullies you?*

START WRITING. With no thought or hesitation, begin journaling about what it is that's "bullying" you. This isn't about the bullying you experienced in high school (although it could be); it's about revealing what's going on with you now, today – money, imperfection, love or the lack thereof. Any topic, any feeling, anything goes. What's weighing on your mind and heart?

GET CREATIVE. If words won't come, do a drawing. If you can't draw, write a poem. If you're not poetic, make origami. Pencil, crayon, watercolors -- you name it. Let that piece of paper express how you're feeling right now.

EMBRACE IMPERFECTION. Don't worry about spelling or punctuation. If you don't miss a couple of commas and you don't mix up a few "you're" and "yours," you're/your over-thinking this. Simply get those imperfect feelings that are in your heart and soul onto the page...imperfectly.

DON'T SIGN IT. Leave it anonymous. We want to know your story but not your name...because what bullies you does not define you.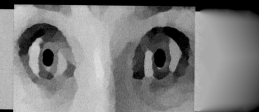

AmAnonymous.org for information on submitting your

Made in the USA
San Bernardino, CA
13 November 2014